COMMITTED

TO CHRIST

Six Steps to a Generous Life

Small Group Leader Guide

by Frank Ramirez

ABINGDON PRESS
Nashville

Committed to Christ
Six Steps to a Generous Life

Small Group Leader Guide
by Frank Ramirez

Based on an original work by Bob Crossman

This book is printed on acid-free, elemental chlorine-free paper.

ISBN 978-14267-4353-5

12 13 14 15 16 17 18 19 20 21—10 9 8 7 6 5 4 3 2
MANUFACTURED IN THE UNITED STATES OF AMERICA

CONTENTS

INTRODUCTION

If you take your beloved car in for an oil change and the mechanic tells you there's no tread on your tires, the transmission fluid is leaking, and your battery is dying, you'll realize you can't fix just one thing. You've got a whole network of interrelated problems that need solving at the same time. Or you could just change the oil, ignoring the sputtering and rattling until your car breaks down for good.

In recent years there have been clear signs that stewardship is on the wane in this beloved church of Jesus Christ. In the past, the solution generally has been to take the church in for an oil change—but in Bob Crossman's stewardship program, Committed to Christ: Six Steps to a Generous Life, we learn a better way.

In the life of the Christian disciple and the church, everything is connected. There's no use thinking that all we need is a little arm-twisting to meet our budgets. We need to see the whole range of shaking, rattling, and rolling, so we can diagnose the problem and fix it.

We need a church dedicated to daily prayer, daily Bible reading, and faithful worship attendance. We need a church prepared to witness, give as an integrated part of Christian life, and perform hands-on service in the name of Jesus.

Committed to Christ invites all of us to be fully committed to Jesus in all aspects of life. In this program, everyone—the young; the old; those engaged in a fulfilling career; those at loose ends, uncertain of what awaits them; those going through times of crisis; and those going through life on auto pilot—will be confronted with the idea that Jesus might actually expect more, and we can respond prayerfully and honestly on a card that offers a wide range of commitments.

The Importance of Small Groups

Much of the Committed to Christ program, as you might expect, will be introduced in worship. In addition, there will be advanced planning, banners, mailings, and other program activities, to take advantage of individual talents.

However, the small group has to be at the forefront of a program such as this one. The small group is where hearts and minds meet. Small groups serve as the yeast, causing the whole lump of dough to rise. Small groups are where you find people committed to the church—the ones for whom Sunday worship is not enough. Small group members give their time and interest to the work of Jesus. They want more. Committed to Christ is about being *more* of a disciple, *more* of a Christian, doing *more* in the name of Christ, and receiving more blessings.

This is where you come in. You are the leader of a small group. Together with your group, you will work to discover and celebrate the joys that come with abundant Christian living.

Each week in worship, a commitment card will be distributed among all in attendance. These cards invite individuals to choose from a wide range of responses to that week's theme: commitment to Christ, prayer, Bible reading, worship, witness, financial giving, and service. Plan your small group sessions so the group is studying the same theme that will be emphasized in worship that week. Then, when the theme is lifted up in worship, your group members already will have explored the theme prior to the time the cards are distributed. Group members are prepared, then, to make more committed choices and to understand why being a Christian means saying yes to God with joy.

To be sure that your group is aware of and using the commitment cards, get a stack of the cards from the church office—for the introductory week, plus the six weeks of the program—and distribute these cards at group sessions. Discuss their importance. Emphasize the role of commitment in the lives of disciples.

In addition to a set of commitment cards, each member of the group will need an *Adult Readings and Study Book,* which serves as the participant book in this small group study. In this book, Bob Crossman introduces the program themes in a friendly, accessible, and clear way. Your task, as leader, is to guide your small group through the book. Some of your group members will faithfully read the week's chapter prior to arrival. Some may not. This leader guide gives you a step-by-step framework to guide everyone, regardless of how much they have prepared, through each important topic.

Session Plans

This Leader Guide includes a session plan for a preliminary week on commitment to Christ, followed by session plans for the six weeks of the program on the themes of prayer, Bible reading, worship, witness, financial giving, and service.

Each session plan begins with a list of goals, followed by activities in three categories: preparing for the session, leading the session, and wrapping up.

Preparing for the Session

This section, intended for you as the leader, includes guidelines for personal preparation as well as biblical and historical insights for enrichment. There's also a list of materials you should gather before the session begins.

Leading the Session

Designed to help you during the group session itself, this section begins with an opening prayer. You will then find study questions that you can use to introduce the topic, followed by an opening activity that invites group members to use their hands and other alternative learning approaches. These activities are meant to be fun but have been designed to meet the goals of the session.

The opening activities are followed by the heart of the session: Exploring the Bible and Exploring the Book. Here you will find lots of help, including insights, discussion questions, and Scripture passages.

Note that we are providing more discussion questions than study groups can process. This is not a test in which every question must be answered! Please feel free to choose the questions that seem best suited to the interests and needs of your group.

Wrapping Up

This section guides you in closing the session. It begins by linking learnings with commitment cards, worship, and life at church and at home. The session concludes with a closing prayer.

Your Role

As a leader, expect to listen as much as to speak. Take your planning seriously, and read this book early enough in the week so that you have plenty of time to hunt down materials.

Feel free, once the session is underway, to abandon your planning and let the session go in unexpected directions. On the other hand, recognize that sometimes you have to be the traffic cop, especially when you sense that one person may be hijacking the sessions, or that someone is making comments that are too personal or unhelpful.

Perhaps your most important role is as timekeeper. As the poet Andrew Marvell wrote centuries ago:

> But at my back I always hear
> Time's winged chariot hurrying near.

Respect your group by starting promptly, and end at the appointed time.

We pray that these group sessions will help you develop fully devoted and committed disciples of Christ.

An Invitation to Follow Christ

Goals

- Covenant with other group members to work through the study in good faith.
- Discover that being a Christian begins with choosing to be a committed follower and disciple of Jesus Christ.
- Understand in advance the six steps to be taken over the next six sessions.

Remember, the Holy Spirit may have additional goals. Be aware; stay attentive. Listen. React. Respond. But also be ready to lead the group back on track if you get lost in an unprofitable tangent.

Preparing for the Session

Personal Preparation

Begin your preparation by praying as a group leader for God's guidance and for the encouragement and strength of the Holy Spirit. Also bring before God a concern from your activities that day.

Set aside time to read the *Adult Readings and Study Book* (hereafter referred to simply as "the book") from beginning to end—or at the very least the first three or four chapters. It is important to see clearly how Bob Crossman organizes and presents information, and to see how the chapters fit together.

Take time to read thoroughly the opening chapter, "An Invitation to Follow Christ." It helps if you read this section twice, once each on separate days. During the second reading, highlight and mark up the chapter in a way that is helpful to you. In between the two readings, study this session plan in the Leader Guide.

Prayerfully consider how important this program and small group study will be for you, for group members, and for the church. Consider how important it is for you to set a good example.

Gather the items listed under "Materials" early in the week before the session. Do not put this off until the last minute.

Enrichment

John 10:1–10
In this passage Jesus describes himself as the Good Shepherd. Psalm 23 describes the Lord as our shepherd. In the days of the Old Testament, kings were expected to rule in the manner of a shepherd who had the well-being of the people at heart, rather than as an autocrat. Jesus, the Good Shepherd, is our guide—not a convenient proof for our prejudices, backup for our political convictions, or prop for our arguments. We are following Jesus; Jesus is not following us.

Deuteronomy 6:4–9
This passage is known as the Shema, from the Hebrew word for "Hear!" God's people are called to hear and repent, to teach their children, and even to wear this central affirmation of faith. God is one, and we are to love God with all our being. When Jesus was asked to identify the greatest commandment, he actually chose two, and this is one of them. It is one of the foundations of our faith.

Leviticus 19:18b
This is the other foundation, also chosen by Jesus as the essential law. Our faith is both vertical and horizontal. That Jesus calls us to have a

relationship with God based on love—that's the vertical. But Jesus also calls us to have a relationship with our neighbors, also based on love. That's the horizontal. And for those who remember Jesus' parable of the Good Samaritan, the definition of neighbor is broad enough to include our enemies!

Materials

- Refreshments for the opening session
- Materials to make "footprints" to be used in the opening activity and during the next six weeks, including posterboard or other stiff white cardboard, markers, and scissors
- Tape or pins to fasten the covenant and the group members' footprints to the wall
- Photocopies of opening and closing unison prayers for group members, as needed
- Six celebration candles
- Poster paper for writing down interests
- Copies of the covenant used in the closing

LEADING THE SESSION

As you begin your time together, invite group members to turn off cell phones and other electronic devices (unless a particular group member must be available in case of emergency).

Without calling attention to whether group members have brought a Bible to today's session, invite them to bring one to subsequent sessions. Emphasize that you would like group members to bring whatever translation they like best, and ideally several different translations will be shared with the group.

Gather group members into one comfortable space in the meeting area. Allow time for brief introductions and a one-sentence statement of what each would like to get from this series of sessions. Review briefly some of the goals and activities of the Committed to Christ program (see Introduction, above), of which this small group study is a crucial part. Then call the group together for worship, passing out photocopies of the opening prayer.

Opening Prayer

Leader: In Jesus is life, and the life is the light of all people. The light shines in the darkness, and the darkness cannot overcome it. (Based on John 1:4)

Light all six candles. Pray aloud:

All: Heavenly Father, we come to the light of your Son, Jesus Christ, our Savior. In the past, each of us has had opportunities to follow Jesus. Yet we know there is so much more we can do, that we might have not just life, but abundant life. We long to be committed to Christ in all we say and do, not only because our lives will be enriched but because your name will be glorified. Bless us during our time together, and let your presence be felt in the written Word, in the spoken word, and in the breath of your Holy Spirit, present always among us. Amen.

Introducing the Topic

Invite group members to name their passions—sports, hobbies, avocations, and so on. List these on poster paper. Discuss some of the following questions:

- What do you really enjoy in life?
- Where is your passion?
- What gets you excited?
- What place do these interests have in your life?
- How much time do they take during the week?

Opening Activity

Pass out posterboard, markers, and scissors. Invite group members to help each other trace six copies of their shoes, three of the left and three of the right. Cut out the footprints and write the names of the six book chapters on them. The chapters are:

1. Let Us Pray
2. Reading the Bible Daily
3. Let Us Go to the House of the Lord
4. You Shall Be My Witnesses
5. Financial Giving
6. Hands-on Service in Jesus' Name

Group members may individualize or decorate their footprints as they choose. Each person should stack and set their footprints to the side as you gather the group back together. After the session, collect all the remaining footprints, for use in future sessions.

Exploring the Bible

Read aloud Deuteronomy 6:4–9, a passage about loving God that Jesus quoted as being important. This passage, which includes the prayer known as the Shema, calls for believers to write down the prayer and to wear it wherever they go.

Share some of the information you learned in the Enrichment section. Discuss:

- What percentage of your being do you think you use to follow God?
- What has God done for you?
- When you say you love God, are you really saying you love what God does for you?
- What place does love have in your relationship with your creator?
- In what ways do you demonstrate, by what you say, do, wear, or serve, the nature of your belief?

The other verse Jesus quoted as being important defines our relationship with other people. You are probably very familiar with the phrase "You shall love your neighbor as yourself," from Leviticus 19:18. After reading it aloud, discuss:

- What does it mean to love your neighbor as yourself? Do you have a high enough opinion of yourself to make this worthwhile?

- What was the context when Jesus quoted this verse?
- Is it easier to love God or your neighbor or yourself?
- Do you think that following these commandments would increase your commitment to Christ? Why or why not?

Invite someone to read John 10:1–10 aloud. Discuss:
- What do you think Jesus meant in this passage by the word *life*?
- What did Jesus mean by *abundantly*?
- To whom did Jesus come to give life and to give it abundantly?
- Why do you think Jesus did not offer this abundant life automatically?

Exploring the Book

Write down on poster paper the six steps of the journey your group is about to undertake together: Prayer, Bible Reading, Worship, Witness, Financial Giving, Service. Remind the group of these steps and post the list during the following discussion.

In the book, Bob Crossman tells the story of a three-legged dog in An Invitation to Follow Christ. The dog, though wounded, welcomes folks to church. Discuss:
- How are you wounded? Share as you feel comfortable.
- What are your strengths?
- What are your weaknesses?

Bob Crossman talks about how he covenanted with a friend to make changes in his life.
- What were some of the changes Bob Crossman made?
- What changes might you make in your life?
- What is the importance of working with others to make changes in your life?

Ask a group member to read aloud the second half of John 10:10. Then turn the group's attention to the questions of John Wesley in An

Invitation to Follow Christ. Write "Altogether Christian" on one sheet of poster paper and "Almost Christian" on another sheet. Discuss the following questions and write responses on the two sheets of poster paper.

- What does it mean to be "almost Christian"?
- What does it mean to be "altogether Christian"?
- Where do you stand on this spectrum?

WRAPPING UP

Remind group members that they are empowered to set a good example of commitment as they prayerfully consider how they will respond to commitment cards at worship on Sunday.

Pass out printed copies of the covenant that is printed at the end of this session plan. Read the covenant aloud together, then post it in the meeting room. You and the group will be referring to it and using it in subsequent sessions.

Enjoy a time of refreshments. Refreshments are also specified for the final session. If you wish to have refreshments every week of the series make sure you allow a little extra time so the session is not cut short. Invite members to volunteer for refreshments. Take a census of dietary restrictions and needs among the group members.

Closing Prayer
Read in unison.

One in Christ, we come together, ready to grow as God gives us the strength. We hope, each in our turn, to inspire and be inspired, to speak and listen, to pray and be prayed for. May the seeds planted by our group bear rich fruit not only in our congregation but throughout the Body of Christ. This we pray, not for our benefit, but that your name may be glorified, Light of Light, True God, Eternal Savior. Amen.

COVENANT

I prayerfully covenant to take my attendance seriously. Our goal is to strengthen our commitment to Christ. Commitment includes accountability and responsibility. Unless there is a truly unforeseen emergency, I plan to attend each session.

I prayerfully covenant to read each chapter prior to the session, to take notes in my copy of the book, and to be prepared to take part in all discussions.

I prayerfully covenant to bring a Bible to each session.

I prayerfully covenant to share honestly with my sisters and brothers, to say what's on my mind, and to recognize that mine is not the only opinion.

I prayerfully covenant to respect everyone in the group and to direct my comments toward an opinion or stance, not against another person.

I prayerfully covenant to listen carefully, hear what is being said, allow others to finish their comments, and recognize that Jesus Christ is present in all of us.

I prayerfully covenant to leave what is said within the room, maintain confidentiality, and help create a safe place for people to discuss, wonder, share, speculate, and praise.

I prayerfully covenant to leave the group in the hands of God, and to allow the Holy Spirit to work as it chooses.

I give thanks now and always to God the Creator, to our Lord and Savior Jesus Christ, and to the Holy Spirit, present and active. Amen.

1.
LET US PRAY

Goals

- Define prayer as a simple and direct way to talk with God.
- Recognize the importance of daily, disciplined prayer.
- Discover the value of both scripted and unscripted prayer.
- Covenant with each other to set aside time each day for prayer.

PREPARING FOR THE SESSION

Personal Preparation

Take time for personal prayer. Pray for God's guidance as you lead and for the members of the group. Also, bring before God a concern from that day.

In the *Adult Readings and Study Book,* read through Chapter 1, Let Us Pray, twice, once each on separate days. In between, read this corresponding session plan in your *Leader Guide.* During the second reading of the book chapter, highlight and mark it up in a way that is helpful to you.

Take a few moments to consider the levels of commitment offered when commitment cards are passed out at worship. (See *Program Guide With CD-ROM.*) Make a note of how you think you will respond.

Set aside appropriate time to make "Prayer Lib" sheets. (See below.)

Gather materials as listed below.

Photocopy opening and closing prayers for use by the group.

Enrichment

1 Chronicles 29:11
The books of Chronicles presents biblical history in a different light from the books of Samuel and Kings. This passage will be examined more closely in session five, but here the words of prayer and praise that identify God as the source of everything are emphasized.

Matthew 6:5–13
When Jesus' disciples asked him for a prayer, he gave this response, known generally as the Lord's Prayer. Many think that the early Christians did not just pray this prayer but used each clause as an opening for extended prayer. The prayer ties together praise of God and our relationship with each other in a series of petitions.

1 Corinthians 12:12–18
The apostle Paul writes to the Corinthian house churches and likens their ethnic and cultural diversity to differences in the parts of a human body. Just as each part of the body has a different function, so each believer has different talents and gifts to share. As such the members, or body parts, are not independant. Each of us is integral to the wholeness of the Body of Christ.

Materials

- First footprints ("Let Us Pray") made in introductory session
- Tape or pins to fasten the footprints to the wall

- Copies of "Prayer Lib" page at the end of this chapter for group members
- Six celebration candles
- Simple magnets
- Glue
- 3 x 5" cards
- Scissors
- Markers of various colors
- Copies of the opening and closing prayers, as needed

LEADING THE SESSION

Opening Prayer

Light the first of the six candles. Pray aloud:

Leader: Let us pray, sisters and brothers. In the name of God, who is worthy of all praise, let us pray.

All: God of power, God of glory and might, bless us, your children, as we gather together in your name. Open our hearts that we might see, even though we approach with awe, that we are not strangers to you. You welcome us and invite us to pray, simply and together, in your name. Amen.

Introducing the Topic

Invite group members to share any brief comments they may have had about the previous week's session. Then note, as suggested by the opening activity, that this week's topic is prayer—specifically, daily prayer.

Pass out copies of this week's commitment card. Discuss the levels of prayer commitment described—what each level involves and how it might change the lives of group members who make that commitment.

Opening Activity

Pass out copies of the "Prayer Libs" template, along with colored markers. Ask, "Have you ever played the game Mad Libs? Here's a little exercise called Prayer Libs. Each of you will create a prayer by filling in the blanks. Aim for:
- Simplicity
- Clarity
- Brevity

After the prayers are finished, ask group members to read their prayers if they feel comfortable doing so.

Exploring the Bible

The words in 1 Chronicles 29:11 are part of a beautiful prayer by King David when he dedicated the work that would begin on the Temple after his death. These are words of praise.

First, read verse 11 together. (If group members do not share the same Bible translation, then "line" the text: The leader recites a phrase, the group repeats the same phrase, and so on.) Then consider some of the following questions. The prayer begins by praising God for greatness, power, glory, victory, and majesty.
- Discuss the meaning of these words as they apply to God.
- When, if ever, have you experienced these attributes of God?
- Describe and compare your experiences of prayer. The prayer in verse 11 continues by recognizing God as Lord of everything in heaven and on earth.
- Invite group members to name things, places, and people in heaven and on earth.
- After each item is named, recite together: "We praise you, Lord of heaven and earth, for _____."

David, the author of the prayer, is king of Israel, yet he emphasizes that God is the Lord of everything, including those in power.
- Name your allegiances: national, cultural, and ethnic identity; clubs, organizations, sports teams, hobbies, passions, and avocations that you consider important.

- As each is named, pray together: "But yours is the kingdom, O Lord, and you are exalted as head above all."

Ask the group to review the allegiances they have named. Consider the following questions:
- Have you ever found your allegiances to be in conflict with your discipleship?
- Have you ever found yourself embarrassed by expressing your faith in public?
- When have you experienced public prayer? Were you taking part in it or observing? What difference might that have made in how you responded?

Read together 1 Corinthians 12:1–18. Discuss:
- What does it mean to be a member of the Body of Christ?
- What part of the body are you?
- What are your strengths?
- What are your weaknesses?
- Which gifts have you used for the work of Christ?
- Which gifts have you not used for Christ?
- Describe the gifts of others that have strengthened you.
- Describe times when others have told you they were strengthened by your gifts.

The final biblical text is the familiar Lord's Prayer, found in Matthew 6:5–13. At this time, pray together the words of the Lord's Prayer as they appear in the Bible. Discuss:
- What portions of the prayer praise God?
- What portions are requests? What is requested? Who benefits from the requests?
- What portions of the prayer seem to include tasks for us?
- What is important about each part of this prayer?
- Is there a part of the prayer you do not understand?
- Are there parts of the prayer, as you discuss it, that seem to be understood differently by different members of the group?

Exploring the Book

Examine some of the prayers described by Bob Crossman in the book, and explore ways in which these prayers offer insight into how we should pray and how simply we should pray. He suggests that, just as someone might have an extremely powerful computer but uses it only for simple tasks, so too we have an extremely powerful resource in prayer which we rarely use to its fullest effect.

In Chapter 1, Crossman notes that he prays fifteen minutes a day and encourages us to "step out of the puddle and into the ocean," to quote Adam Hamilton ("Remembering True North," sermon, 14 July 2002). He lifts up the Gospel text that precedes the Lord's Prayer and tells a funny story about a "Say What?" prayer.

- What is the author saying about "fancy" prayer?
- What does Jesus ask us to avoid in prayer?
- Does any of this remind you of how you were taught to pray?
- Have you ever heard a "Say What?" prayer? What were the circumstances?

Read aloud, or ask a group member to read aloud, the Richard Foster quotation in Chapter 1.

- Invite participants to rephrase the author's definition of "simple prayer."
- As a group work, based on this first chapter and your own experience, define simple prayer together. In the spirit of simplicity, try to use as many one-syllable words as you can.

The author also shares a story and prayer centered on a Haitian woman who struggles with severe illness and difficulties.

- What was your reaction to this story and prayer?
- What lessons does the author draw from the story? What lessons do you draw?
- How can this example strengthen your own prayer life?

The author suggests a memory aid for prayer using the acronym

BLESS. Consider and discuss
- What does each letter stand for?
- What parts of BLESS do you find in the Lord's Prayer?
- What parts do you already use in your own prayers?
- What parts might you consider adding to your own prayers?

Close this part of the session by asking group members if there is anything they underlined or highlighted that has not been covered in the session. Ask them to lift up those items and invite comments from other group members.

WRAPPING UP

Remind the group of the covenant they made last week (a copy should still be posted on the wall of the meeting area). Then spend a few moments reviewing the commitment card that will be used during the upcoming worship service. Today's commitment card, like today's session, will be about prayer.

Ask the group whether prayer is a topic they would like to explore in greater depth and detail after the program. Suggested resources can be found on the CD-ROM that accompanies the *Committed to Christ Program Guide,* under "Tools and Helps."

Finally, have group members post the first of their six footsteps to the wall, with the words Daily Prayer written on it.

Closing Prayer

Close the session with sentence prayers, offered by group members in no particular order. A sentence prayer is a prayer that is one sentence long. No fancy language allowed. The group leader will close with "Amen."

Prayer Libs

_____ ,
(Whom you are addressing your prayer to)

I come before you to praise you for

_____ .
(Something about God, your world, the events of the day)

I want to thank you for

_____ .
(Something you are thankful for)

_____ , you are like
(Whom you are addressing)

_____ .
(What God is like, in your opinion)

I am concerned about _____ .
(Whom or what you are concerned about)

I need _____ .
(What you need)

Please _____ .
(What you want God to do about it)

Help me to _____ .
(Something you wish to accomplish)

_____ , you are
(Whom you are addressing)

_____ .
(A reason God should be praised)

Amen.

2.
READING THE BIBLE DAILY

Goals

- Commit to daily Bible reading.
- Appreciate the Bible as essential to the life of a committed Christian disciple.
- Link daily Bible reading with daily prayer.

PREPARING FOR THE SESSION

Personal Preparation

As a follow-up to the previous session on prayer, encourage group members by phone or email during the week to pray God's guidance for the group as you prepare for this week's session.

Read Chapter 2 in the book carefully, and take time to look up the Scripture references. Follow by reading this session plan in the *Leader Guide*. Then return to Chapter 2 of the book and make notes to correspond with suggestions in the guide, as well as your own ideas for this week's session.

If you have the time and inclination (or know of a group member who does), consider finding photographs of Erik Weihenmayer and the many mountains he climbed. Put together a PowerPoint presentation or slide show and project it at gathering time or during discussion of the book.

Make sure you leave time to gather all the materials needed for this session.

Enrichment

2 Timothy 3:15–17
In this short passage the apostle Paul, imprisoned and likely facing execution, charges Timothy to rely on Scripture, which he has known since childhood, as the foundation of belief and ministry. It is worth noting that at this time in history, there was no one accepted list of scriptural books. Various Jewish groups had different lists of inspired Scriptures, and of course much of the New Testament had not even been written yet, much less collected together in one place.

James 1:19–25
James (Jacob), the brother of Jesus, was the leader of the Jerusalem church until his murder by religious authorities in A.D. 62. This letter, written to believers scattered around the empire, emphasizes the practical nature of Christian faith—and indeed, the fact that for faith to be real, it must be applied in our lives.

Exodus 20:1–17
This passage contains the Ten Words, as they are sometimes known, or more familiarly, the Ten Commandments. Although different faith traditions divide the passage in different ways, these commandments represent the way God's Word provides not a negative series of prohibitions but a positive series of boundaries that make life safe and secure.

Where did the Bible come from?
Neither the first Christians nor the teachers in the synagogue could have put their hands on a Bible as we know it. For many centuries the Torah scroll, containing the first five books of our Bible, was Scripture.

Even in Jesus' day there was great disagreement about which Hebrew writings were inspired.

Later, these Hebrew Scriptures were translated into Greek and established as a canon for Jews throughout the Roman Empire and for the early Christians. Included were the books we know as the Apocrypha, which is why for centuries all Christians considered these books to be sacred.

The Hebrew Bible as we know it was established, according to tradition, at the Council of Jamnia, held around the year A.D. 90. This list was adopted by reformers fifteen hundred years later.

Christians did not have a New Testament for decades, even centuries. Only gradually did the Gospels, letters, and other writings coalesce into a canon. The community of faith, under the guidance of the Holy Spirit, achieved consensus carefully and prayerfully over time.

Finally, scrolls were replaced by the codex, which consisted of lambskin sheets bound together in what we would recognize as a book; and only then, when all the books of Scripture as we know it were finally gathered together between two covers, could one finally speak of a Bible.

Materials

- Second footprints ("Reading the Bible Daily") made in introductory session
- Tape or pins to fasten the footprints to the wall
- Six celebration candles
- Poster paper or large post-notes and markers
- Photocopied opening and closing prayers, as needed

LEADING THE SESSION

Opening Prayer

Light the first and second of the six candles.
Invite a group member to read aloud Psalm 119:105–11.

Prayer of Blessing

All: As we open the book with the words of life,

Open our eyes to the reading,

Open our hearts to your pleading,

Open our minds to your leading.

Amen.

Introducing the Topic

Open by reviewing the previous session on prayer. Spend two or three minutes in discussion.

- How did it go?
- Did it help to pray on a regular basis?
- Did you spend some prayer time listening to God as well as speaking?

Introduce today's topic of Bible reading. Compare the Bibles brought by group members.

- Which translations do you use?
- What are the features?
- What do you look for in a Bible?

Opening Activity

Gather together in a comfortable setting. Consider the following question: What Bible story from your childhood is the most vivid?

Choose one story from those suggested by group members, and together retell the story as fully as you can, filling in gaps for each other. Then lay out sheets of poster paper or other large drawing paper, and pass out art supplies. Quickly draw large comic-strip versions of the story. Don't worry about technical skill. Stick figures are fine. Fix the drawings to the wall and discuss.

Exploring the Bible

Today, buying a Bible is more a matter of making consumer choices, such as attractive binding, easy-to-read type, illustrations, and helpful notes. But the very existence of this single volume containing a whole library of books might cause us to forget that the earliest Christians had no access to the book we call the Bible. For example, the part we now call the New Testament hadn't been written or, later, hadn't been collected together yet. Share some of the information from the Enrichment section, "Where did the Bible come from?"

2 Timothy 3:15–17
This is part of the apostle Paul's advice to a younger colleague named Timothy, who had learned Bible stories from his mother and grandmother. Listen carefully as one group member reads aloud 1 Timothy 3:15–17. Then discuss:
- When and how did you first learn about the teachings of the Bible?
- When, if ever, did you start reading the Bible on your own?
- Does part of 1 Timothy 3:15–17 speak especially to you? Which part? Why?
- Have you ever read or heard a passage from the Scriptures that you found hard to accept? Where? Why?

Exodus 20:1–17
This passage includes what we call the Ten Commandments, delivered by God to Moses on Mount Sinai. Some complain that our faith includes too many "Thou shalt nots," but I would suggest that these commandments create boundaries that make truly free living possible. Bob Crossman states: "We are not simply invited to read the Bible; we are invited to accept its teachings."
- Which commandments define our relationship with God?
- Which commandments define our relationships with each other?
- How could these commandments improve the quality of living in our society?

- Which of these commandments are largely ignored by people?
- Which seem hardest to keep?
- Which is most difficult for you?
- Which is easiest?
- What does it mean to take the Ten Commandments seriously?

Bible Reading in Our Lives

Concerning the state of your own relationship with Scripture, discuss the following:

- How often, and for how long, do you engage in Bible reading?
- Do you read the Bible only when you want something?
- Are there parts of the Bible you feel well acquainted with?
- What part of the Bible would you like to know more about?
- What steps would you like to take in reading the Bible? Bob Crossman reminds us in his closing prayer that God has given us 10,000 minutes in a week. Actually, there are 10,080! That's an extra eleven minutes a day (with three left over for brushing your teeth on Tuesday).
- How many minutes do you sleep each week?
- How many minutes do you work each week?
- How many do you watch television, read, or engage in other forms of entertainment?
- If you can covenant to use roughly eleven minutes a day for Bible reading, what approach would you like to use? (For example, select certain books or passages; engage in a deliberate reading program; read daily; read at a particular time.)

Exploring the Book

If you were able to assemble some pictures of Erik Weihenmayer's mountain climbing, project them now. Whether you have pictures or not, ask a group member to read aloud the book paragraphs having to do with Erik. Discuss the importance of trust and listening when it comes to God's word.

- What mountains have you faced in your lifetime?
- When facing these mountains, have you relied on yourself, on another person, on God's word, or on God's spirit for guidance?

Crossman suggests that the letter of James includes many insights on practical Christianity.

- Have a group member read James 1:19–25, then ask the group to rephrase the passage in their own words.
- Is there a nonverbal way to express what the passage states?

The author of James uses the comic image of people who look in the mirror and immediately forget what they look like, then compares this to people who hear God's word but don't do what it says.

- Has this happened in your life?
- When have you done something when you knew better?

Crossman tells a story about applicants for the job of Morse code operator.

- Was there a time if your life when God spoke clearly to you, but you didn't understand or act on what you were told?
- Has there been a time when, like the Morse code operator, you did understand and acted on what you were told?

The author tells two stories, one about a boy who was disappointed on his sixteenth birthday, and another about a woman who yelled "pig" at an oncoming motorist. Briefly retell these stories. Compare these two stories with the passage from the letter of James.

- How do these two stories illustrate the Scripture?
- What lessons have you learned, the hard way?
- When have you benefited, either from Scripture, life, or the advice of others, by seriously considering what you were told?.
- Have others taken seriously the lessons you tried to give?

James W. Moore, in the concluding story, tells how the Cross is identified as our measuring stick for truth.

Are there crosses you have encountered in your experience that have provided a light in dark places or a compass when you were lost?

What were these things? How did they demonstrate the truth of Scripture?

WRAPPING UP

Share the words of covenant you put together during the initial session.

Ask group members how they can encourage others outside of the group when it's time to respond to the commitment cards this Sunday for Bible reading.

Claim this second step on the Committed to Christ journey. Ask the group to select Bible reading partners for accountability. Commit to contacting each other daily via phone, e-mail, text, or other means to see how your Bible reading progresses.

Point out to group members that the Common English Bible translation and Web site are helpful resources for Bible study. In addition, a number of plans are available for reading the entire Bible over the course of one year. Daily Scriptures are available at www.MinistryMatters.com, as well as in a variety of popular apps.

Are you a better listener than reader? Ask the group to consider listening to an audio Bible instead of a printed Bible. You can purchase one at a bookstore, or download a free version from the Internet.

Ask each group member to claim the second of their six footsteps, with the words Daily Prayer written on it, and fasten the footstep on the wall beside the others.

Closing Prayer
Read in unison

Jesus, Savior, Lord, Redeemer, grant us this abundant life—through commitment to you, through prayer, and through daily Bible reading. Amen.

3.
LET US GO TO THE HOUSE OF THE LORD

Goals

- Commit to the habit of regular church attendance.
- Learn that being an active disciple is not an option but an expectation.
- Develop strategies that encourage others to attend regularly.

PREPARING FOR THE SESSION

Personal Preparation

Pray for God's guidance as you prepare for this week's session. Pray for each group member in turn, that God's will may be done in their lives.

In the book, read carefully Chapter 3: Worship, and take time to look up the Scripture references. Follow by reading this corresponding session plan in the leader guide, including the Enrichment section. Return to Chapter 3 and make notes to correspond with suggestions in the session plan as well as your own ideas for this week's session.

Make copies of the word puzzle at the end of this chapter.

This week's commitment card will invite you to become an active, prayerfully prepared participant in worship among other options. Which level of commitment are you prepared to make? How will you present the levels of commitment to group members?

Make sure you leave time before the session to gather all needed materials.

Enrichment

Matthew 7:15–20
This short passage is part of a larger section known as the Sermon on the Mount. Jesus introduces his interpretation of the scriptural Law, which focuses as much on intent as on literal observance of the commandments. The point here is that it's not enough to put on a good show when it comes to our faith. We are known by the fruit we produce, meaning good works.

Ephesians 5:18b-20
In this letter, Paul writes to believers who live in an ancient city that is a center of the mystery religions, in which initiates are constantly seeking to enter into a new inner circle of secret knowledge. Paul prays that the Ephesian Christians can, through the Holy Spirit, come to know the depth of God's love and power in their worship together. He shares with us the pattern of worship in the synagogue service, which was the foundation for worship in the early Christian church. For the Christian, there are no hoops to jump through or secret circles to enter. It's enough to praise God for being God.

Leviticus 19:14
The nineteenth chapter of Leviticus, like the letter of James, insists that the way to be holy is by living in a just relationship with God's people. This prohibition against making fun of or putting barriers in the way of the disabled challenges us to insure that our houses of worship are accessible to all.

Materials

- Footprints made in the introductory session: Let Us Go to the House of the Lord
- Tape or pins to fasten the footprints to the wall

- Six celebration candles
- Photocopies of Word Puzzle
- Pens or pencils for Word Puzzle
- Photocopies of opening and closing prayers, as needed

LEADING THE SESSION

Opening Prayer

Light the first, second, and third of the six candles. Read aloud:

Prayer of Blessing

All: Call us homeward, God of Gathering, to the place where we can worship you together. May we think of your church with longing, and to our return with gladness. This we pray in your name. Amen.

Introducing the Topic

Open by allowing group members a couple of minutes to check in with Bible reading partners. Recommit to checking in on a daily basis. Discuss how easy or how hard it has been to keep up with commitments.

- What changes, if any, have you had to make to your daily routine?
- Did it help to check in with someone on a daily basis?
- Did you rush through Bible reading, or were you able to be more thoughtful?

Discuss your earliest memories of worship, including best and worst experiences. Discuss some elements of your church's present worship service and how a newcomer might respond to these. Discuss worship elements that keep you coming, as well as some you may not like as much.

Today's session is about the importance of making worship an integral part of your life. Bob Crossman admits that in this session, he may be "preaching to the choir," since if people are present in church it is likely they also are actively involved in worship. But this session is about more than just going to church; it's about making the transition from consumer to contributor. The challenge for us, in other words, is more a matter of quality than quantity.

Pass out copies of this week's commitment card, on the topic of worship, and review the levels of commitment listed. Ask group members to consider stepping up their level of commitment.

Opening Activity

Distribute copies of the Word Puzzle (see below) as well as pens and pencils. Allow five minutes or so for the group to solve these. Participants may work alone or in groups. After finishing, they can compare answers and correct each other.

Exploring the Bible

In Chapter 3, Crossman states that "becoming a deeply devoted disciple is not just an option; it is an expectation the Lord has of every one who seeks to be a Christian." God cares about us and whether we are taking care of ourselves physically and spiritually.

The chapter includes the words of Jesus from Matthew 7:16–20 in the Living New Testament version. Regardless of which versions group members have brought, invite a group member to read the text out loud. Jesus says in Matthew 7:16–20 that sooner or later trees that do not produce fruit are cut down.

- How do you interpret this passage, not just for the next life but also for quality of life now? Of course, trees will bear better fruit if tended.
- What "tending" do you require as an individual to bear better fruit?
- What is the result when you attend worship and are actively involved in the life of the church?
- Do you notice a change in yourself or others when this is not the case?

The author points out that those not actively involved in church don't consider themselves bad or evil.

- What do we miss out on when not regularly involved in the life of the church?
- How might we effectively invite others to join us at church?

Ephesians 5:18b-20 is one of several Scriptures in which Paul describes elements of an ideal worship service. Singing is one of these elements, as is teaching.

- When do you feel closest to God?
- What is your favorite element of worship? Is this what draws you week after week?
- Are there elements of worship that do not speak to you? How do they seem to speak to others?

The Scripture passage describes different kinds of singing.

- What kinds of hymns are played at your church? Which are your favorites?
- Would you be willing to forego your favorite hymns in order to encourage attendance by others?
- What associations, if any, do you have between hymns and important events in your life?
- Does any "admonishing" take place in your worship life? What do you think Paul (and the translators) meant by this word?

Read Leviticus 19:14. This nineteenth chapter of Leviticus describes the way God's people become a holy people, and much of it has to do with how we treat those around us. This admonition against mistreating the disabled means that we should insure that every activity of our congregation is open to all.

- What difficulties do you or others encounter when attending worship or other activities of the church?
- Think about what it is like to take part in worship, from the moment one arrives until one leaves.
- Are there portions of the church that are inaccessible to some worshipers?

Exploring the Book

Chapter 3 includes a number of stories. One is about a young priest who notes that many worshipers are satisfied to get by with a minimum amount of effort.

- What is the least you can do to be a true disciple of Jesus? Is it even possible to think in those terms?
- Was there a time when you were content to get a "sprinkling" of Christianity? What changed your mind and heart?

The author compares the motto for Hendrix College ("It takes thirty days to grow a squash. It takes a hundred years to grow a mighty oak") with the ending of Isaiah 61:3 ("that we might become oaks of righteousness"). The passage from Isaiah is the continuation of words Jesus read from the Isaiah scroll when preaching at his home synagogue. Read Isaiah 61:3 aloud. This is the commission Jesus gave himself: to preach to the captives, heal the sick, and proclaim the year of Jubilee.

- What kind of mighty oak of God would you become if you were to do even one third or one fourth of these things?
- Which parts of this commission have you already covenanted to undertake in the first two sessions? Which ones are you already doing, if any?

Crossman asks us what we would need to change in order to make worship a priority. In addition to answering this question, ask yourself what preparation you can do in advance to make worship even more vital and alive.

- How often do you read and study the Scripture text for each week prior to arriving?
- Do you sign up to usher, provide flowers, work in childcare, proofread the bulletins, or in another ways use your skills each Sunday?
- Would you consider calling the pastor or church office to find out what worship tasks need doing?

WRAPPING UP

Remind group members that this week they will be asked to consider a new level of commitment regarding worship. Take a moment to discuss this.

Turn your attention to the original covenant made by group members, which is on display in your meeting room. If there is time, read it aloud again, together. Claim the third step on the Committed to Christ journey. Covenant to explore ways to enrich worship, especially for those who have difficulty getting to worship at regular times. Covenant to reach out to someone who attends irregularly in a friendly and helpful fashion, encouraging them to attend this coming Sunday.

At this time, each group member will fix the third of their six footsteps to the wall—the step with the words Daily Prayer written on it.

Closing Prayer

Heavenly Father, move in our midst, discomfort us, so that we may stop being merely consumers of worship and claim our roles as contributors to worship. Amen.

WORD PUZZLE ANSWER KEY

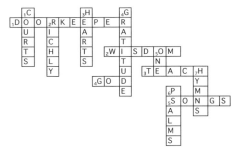

For a day in your courts(D1) is better than a thousand elsewhere. I would rather be a doorkeeper(A1) in the house of my God(A4) than live in the tents of wickedness.

—Psalm 84:10

Let the word of Christ dwell in you richly(D2);teach(A3) and admonish one (D5) another in all wisdom (A2); and with gratitude(D4) in your hearts(D3) sing psalms(D6), hymns(D7), and spiritual songs(A5) to God(A4).

—Colossians 3:16

WORD PUZZLE

Use the clues to fill in the blanks. When you've solved the puzzle, use the answers to fill in the blanks in today's scripture texts, below.

ACROSS
1. URBAN GATE WATCHER
2. THE RESULT OF EXPERIENCE
3. INSTRUCT
4. DEITY
5. CANZONES

DOWN
1. JUDICIAL AND TENNIS
2. AMPLY
3. PINOCLE AND _____
4. THANKFULNESS
5. THREE MINUS TWO
6. ANCIENT HYMNS
7. MODERN PSALMS

For a day in your _____(D1) is better than a thousand elsewhere. I would rather be a _____(A1) in the house of my _____(A4) than live in the tents of wickedness.
—Psalm 84:10

Let the word of Christ dwell in you_____(D2); _____(A3) and admonish _____(D5) another in all _____ (A2); and with _____(D4) in your _____(D3) sing _____(D6), _____(D7), and spiritual _____(A5) to _____(A4)

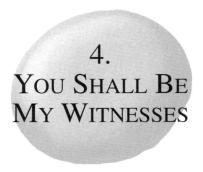

4.
YOU SHALL BE
MY WITNESSES

Goals

- Claim the role of witness as part of your Christian life.
- Understand the nature and meaning of witness.
- Strategize ways and means of witnessing for Jesus.
- Covenant to witness at least once during the course of the week.

PREPARING FOR THE SESSION

Personal Preparation

Pray for God's guidance as you plan this week's session. Pray especially for courage for all in the group, including yourself, as the call to witness seems to be the one dreaded most.

Read this chapter carefully, and take time to look up the Scripture references. Follow by reading the corresponding session plan in this leader guide. Return to the chapter and make notes about suggestions in the session plan, as well as your own ideas for this week's session.

Are you ready to make a real commitment to witnessing? Are you ready to learn what it means to be a witness? Will you be encouraging others in the small group to do the same?

Make sure you leave time before the session to gather needed materials.

Enrichment

Acts 1:7–8
Bob Crossman, author of the *Adult Readings and Study Book,* refers to this text as the last will and testament by Jesus for Christians. Jesus tells the disciples that they needn't become "biblical calculators" who attempt to use Scripture as a calendar to predict the events of the future. Their task is firmly set in the present.

Colosians 4:5–6
The apostle Paul insists that our outward deportment is the way many people know Jesus. See the quotation from the mystic Teresa of Avila, below.

John 8:12
In one of the famous I AM statements of the Gospel of John, Jesus identifies himself as the light of the world, the way all truth is illuminated and revealed.

John 1:40-46
In the Gospel of John, people who encounter Jesus must see the savior for themselves. Then they either get it or they don't. When Jesus calls his first disciples, he gives them a new identity, a new way of looking at themselves, in one case by giving a new name. One early disciple, Andrew, immediately tells Philip, who responds with a smart-aleck remark about Jesus' hometown. Andrew answers by inviting Philip to see for himself, saying simply, "Come and see."

1 Corinthians 3:6–10
Competition has arisen among the house churches of Corinth, based on the question of who was baptized by whom. Paul insists that no one

can claim credit for "catching" new Christians. We are team members, working for the same goal. Several people may have a hand in bringing someone to Christ, but ultimately it is God who performs the wonder.

St. Teresa of Avila

"Christ has no body now on earth but yours, no hands but yours, no feet but yours, yours are the eyes through which Christ's compassion is to look out to the earth, yours are the feet by which He is to go about doing good and yours are the hands by which He is to bless us now."

The Meaning of Witness

The Greek word for witness in the New Testament is the word *marturius,* from which we get our word martyr. For many in the early Christian church, witnessing and martyrdom were directly linked. Living the witness can also have dangerous consequences. Dirk Willems was arrested on May 16, 1569, in the Dutch village of Asperen. His crimes included being baptized as an adult and holding Bible studies in his home. Facing execution at the stake, Willems escaped from prison by tying rags together to form a makeshift rope, after which he lowered himself to the ground and began to run away. A guard ran after him. The spring thaw was barely underway, but Willems managed to run across the ice of a frozen river to freedom. However, the guard chasing him fell through the ice and began to drown. He called out to Willems to save him. Willems turned back and witnessed to his faith by rescuing the guard. He was recaptured and burned at the stake. His execution was botched and Willems suffered terribly. His story has been held up by Christians as an example of the cost of discipleship and how our testifying to the love of Jesus trumps even concerns for our own safety.

Materials

- Bring footprints made in introductory session: "You Shall Be My Witnesses"
- Tape or pins to fasten the footprints to the wall
- Six celebration candles
- Oversized sheets of paper

- Markers
- Scissors
- String
- Poster paper
- Photocopies of unison prayers, as needed

LEADING THE SESSION

Opening Prayer

Light the first, second, third, and fourth of the six candles. Pray aloud:

Unison Prayer of Blessing
    All: Calm our hearts, God who inspires, still our objections, open our minds to the possibility of witnessing to our faith and to you, Lord. The nations are streaming to you. Fill us with your Holy Spirit, that we may witness from our lives, from your Word, from the evidence of creation, and from your people. Amen.

Introducing the Topic

Check in with the group about their commitments to pray, read the Bible, and worship. Then introduce today's session, "You Shall Be My Witnesses." Invite group members to define in one sentence what it means to be a witness for Jesus.

Opening Activity

Provide large poster paper and markers. Invite each group member to draw a large circle and write their name in the circle. Draw more circles, and on each circle write out words such as *family, work, hobbies, book clubs, sports, entertainment,* and other organizations or activities that bring them into contact with people. Inside each circle, write names of people you know through these avenues. Highlight or star the names of those who may not be active in any church.

Cut out the circles. Fasten the circles that have group members' names on them onto a long string, and stretch it across the meeting space. From these name circles, hang more strings and attach each person's circles for other organizations and activities. These are the people your group could witness to.

Exploring the Bible

When you read the letters of Paul, you notice an amazing thing: Though his good news never changes, Paul alters his approach and delivery of that news based on the different backgrounds of each church.

The Galatian church likely included a fair number of Celts. Paul called to mind their cultural background, stating at one point that the Galatians had actually witnessed the crucifixion with their eyes, even though they had done no such thing. That's because Celts experienced stories so deeply and their legends were so alive to them, it was as if they were present when the events happened.

The Ephesians, on the other hand, lived among people who practiced mystery religions, in which secret knowledge was taught to initiates. To these Christians, Paul spoke about the mystical, cosmic battle in which disciples of Christ took part.

Then there were the Philippians, whose citizenship in Philippi also made them citizens of Rome, a city hundreds of miles away that many of them had never seen. As citizens, they had the privileges and responsibilities that went with being a Roman. They took pride in being citizens of what was known, even then, as the eternal city. That's why Paul reminded the Philippians that they were citizens of the true eternal city—heaven—which, like Rome, they had never seen, but to which they were bound by its rules.

- What approach works best for you when introduced to something new by a friend?
- What makes your area, region, or neighborhood different from other places you know?
- For people in your area, what approach to witnessing might work best?
- What approach might work best in other areas where you have lived?

There were several house churches in Corinth that received Paul's letter. Some members of these churches were proud they had been baptized by Jesus. Others took pride in their association with Paul or with St. Apollos, a first-century apostle. Still others may have considered themselves superior by calling theirs the Jesus church. Paul's response in 1 Corinthians 3:6–10 insists that all Christians are part of the same team, each with a different role.

Bob Crossman goes on to mention a Billy Graham Association training event in which he learned that an average convert might experience twenty-four invitations or witnesses before saying yes to the Lord.

- How does this Scripture and idea change the way you might look at your efforts to witness as success or failure?
- When have you been the one to plant, or to water, or to harvest?
- Who fulfilled those roles in your life?

In his story at the end of Chapter 4, Bob Pierson mentions how, in John 1:40-46, Andrew invites Peter to meet Jesus, and Peter invites Nathaniel. Church growth experts will tell you that one person who begins to attend who had no prior connection with the church may lead to other people who do not have a direct and obvious connection as well.

- How often do you invite people to church?
- Has anyone joined the church because of your invitation? Have they in turn invited anyone new?

Exploring the Book

In Chapter 4, Bob Crossman identifies Acts 1:7–8 as the last will and testament of Jesus. Invite a group member to read these verses out loud.

The author states that we must "make the most of every opportunity." He then lists three things we "must not" be. Review these three things, then discuss:

- When have you done a "must not," and what was the result?
- What are some ways we can avoid these errors?

In discussing conversation starters, the author describes how a friend's cross brought about an opportunity to witness to his faith.

- Besides a cross, what could you wear, carry, or keep with you that might be noticed and bring possibilities for discussion?
- Discuss strategies for raising the subject of your church in normal conversations.

There's a story in this chapter about a man who carried around a small mirror, reminding him of John 8:12—how Jesus is the light of the world, and how the man could reflect that light.

- In what ways do your life, your actions, and your words reflect Jesus? In what ways do they not?
- What is your mission field like? What might it be like in the future?
- Whom do you encounter regularly who might benefit from knowing about your church?
- How did you come to attend your current church?
- How did you come to know Jesus?

Invite a group member to read Matthew 10:5–10 from *The Message* translation, printed in Chapter 4 of the *Adult Readings and Study Book.*
Some people call their churches friendly because their friends attend. They visit with their friends before and after church and sit with their friends during worship.

- What steps are important for you to take so that people who walk through your church doors feel welcome?
- To enable you to greet and visit with newcomers in church, are you willing to sacrifice some of the time you spend with people you love and enjoy being with?

In Chapter 4, the author mentions a number of items that might be off-putting to newcomers during their first visit to your church.

- How does your church measure up, in your opinion, with regard to those items?
- Which items can be improved? How?
- How can you make use of social media to reach out to people of all ages?

- Does your church have a Web page? a Facebook page? If not, is there someone in the congregation who could help you set these up and maintain them?

WRAPPING UP

Invite a group member to review Acts 1:7–8 as a reading of Jesus' will—God's legacy to us in Acts.

Ask group members to consider what it will mean to step beyond their comfort level in witnessing for Christ. Remind them about the commitment card they will be reading and signing in church this week on the subject of witness. What level of commitment will they select?

Claim the fourth step on the Committed to Christ journey. Imagine that you are speaking to a stranger or acquaintance about why going to worship would be an exciting activity. Consider the circles you created in the opening activity, and use those circles to decide whom you can invite to worship. Discuss:

- Why is it easier for some people to invite a friend or stranger to a new restaurant rather than to church?
- What is most appealing about your church?
- What are you least comfortable with about your church?

Suggest that each group member write the name of someone they will witness to about your small group and invite to attend. The slips could be put in an empty chair in the middle of the room during the closing prayer.

Ask group members to fasten the fourth of their six footsteps to the wall, a step with the words written on it: "You Shall Be My Witnesses."

Closing Prayer

Invite each group member to lift up, by name or description, someone who is identified in one of the circles attached to their name. Another member of the group will pray out loud for that person, and each time the entire group will conclude with the phrase, "Lord, hear our prayer."

5.
FINANCIAL GIVING

Goals

- Establish financial giving as an integral element of Christian discipleship.
- Identify choices and priorities that present roadblocks to increased giving.
- Encourage group members to raise giving 1% a year to reach a tithing minimum.

PREPARING FOR THE SESSION

Personal Preparation

For many people, the idea of increasing financial gifts to the church, or even discussing them, represents a negative in their relationship with God and the church. Pray for God's guidance in leading this session; in examining your own priorities and motivations with regard to tithing; and in communicating to the group that financial giving to the biblical standard of the tithe is not to "cover" the costs of the church, but is a deep and passionate response to God's love and grace.

Read Chapter 5 twice, carefully, and study the corresponding session plan in this leader in between those readings. Make notes to help you in guiding others.

Consider prayerfully: Are you willing to set an example in biblically based financial giving this coming Sunday? Are you willing to encourage others to do the same?

Make arrangements before the session for the group to have Internet access using a laptop, notebook, or smartphone.

Be sure that you leave time to gather all materials needed for this session.

Enrichment

Deuteronomy 15:1–11; Mark 14:7
In the Mark passage, a woman anoints Jesus with expensive perfume, and onlookers criticize her because she could have sold the perfume and given the money to the poor. Jesus scolds the onlookers because, as he says, we will always have the poor with us. Some people use this text to say that it's no use trying to help the poor, because we will never solve the problem of poverty. However, anyone familiar with the Torah would have realized that Jesus was citing Deuteronomy 15:1–11, which quite clearly states that since God has blessed us, and since there will be poor among us, it is up to us to take care of them. In other words, we have a constant obligation to give to the ministries of the church.

Leviticus 19:9–10; the Book of Ruth
Leviticus 19 is known as the "holy chapter" of the Law. In it, the people are told they are to be holy as God is holy. And the way to be holy is to follow the commandments and to treat people with justice. These verses make it clear that charity is not an option; it is required. God intends that we go through our fields once and then let the poor glean whatever they like afterward. The poor have a right to our money, our goods, and the product of our labors. One can see the result in Ruth. Ruth, a foreigner who is a member of a hated nation, the Moabites, displays the chesed, the steadfast love that is the hallmark of God. She takes advantage of the opportunity to glean in order to support her mother-in-law. This leads in the end to the birth of King David and, ultimately, to Jesus.

Mark 12:41–44

In the Gospel story known as the Widow's Mite, Jesus praises the astounding generosity of a widow, who would have had no regular means of support, for giving all she had. The substantially larger but proportionally smaller gifts given by many richer believers pale in comparison.

Mark 10:17–31

This passage tells a story of the rich young man who pleases Jesus because he knows the commandments. But when Jesus advises the young man to sell all that he has and give it to the poor in order to follow Jesus, the man turns away. Both are saddened by this. Jesus states that it is easier for a camel to go through the eye of a needle than for a rich person to enter heaven. Generally, preachers try to soften this text and talk about a narrow gate into Jerusalem that required traders to lighten the load of their camels in order to enter. There is nothing in the text that suggests this. Instead, Jesus seems to be using hyperbole—or exaggeration, a common storytelling device—to get across the point that our possessions hamper our discipleship.

Materials

- Footprints made in the introductory session: "Financial Giving"
- Tape or pins to fasten the footprints to the wall
- Six celebration candles
- Photocopies of unison prayers, as needed
- Laptops, notebooks, smartphones, or whatever devices are needed to access the Internet in your meeting room

LEADING THE SESSION

Opening Prayer

Light five of the six candles. Pray aloud this prayer of blessing (adapted from the prayer of David in Second Chronicles 29:10-17).

Leader: Blessed are you, O Lord, God of our ancestors, forever and ever. Yours, O Lord, are the greatness, the power, the glory, the victory, and the majesty; for all that is in the heavens and on the earth is yours; yours is the kingdom, O Lord, and you are exalted as head above all.

All: Riches and honor come from you, and you rule over all. In your hand are power and might; and it is in your hand to make great and to give strength to all.

Leader: And now, our God, we give thanks to you and praise your glorious name. But who am I, and what is my people, that we should be able to make this offering? For all things come from you, and of your own have we given you.

All: For we are aliens and transients before you, as were all our ancestors; our days on the earth are like a shadow, and there is no hope. O Lord our God, all this abundance that we have provided to build you a house for your holy name comes from your hand and is all your own.

Leader: I know, my God, that you search the heart and take pleasure in uprightness; in the uprightness of my heart I have freely offered all these things, and now I have seen your people, who are present here, offering freely and joyously to you.

All: Amen.

Introducing the Topic

Spend a short time reflecting together on the opening prayer. King David, represented in Chronicles as being hale and hearty until the time of his passing, organizes the collection of materials and money for the building of the temple after his death.
- Who does King David identify as the source of all that is given to God? Is his statement true for us? Do we take such words seriously?

- How often do we think of our offerings as a privilege more than an obligation?

King David speaks of the joy of being able to give what was God's from the beginning.

- In what ways do we in our use of language identify possessions, land, homes, and lives as "ours" instead of God's?
- How can we change the way we speak so we identify God as the source and owner of all good things?

Pass out copies of this week's commitment card, on financial giving, and discuss with group members the levels of commitment listed. Encourage the group to consider stepping up their level of financial giving, moving closer each year toward the biblical standard of the tithe.

Opening Activity

Taking advantage of the Internet connection that you arranged before class—using either a laptop, notebook, or smartphone—work together to search the Internet for Scriptures in different translations that use the word *tithe* or *tenth*.

- How often does either term appear in the Old Testament?
- How are these terms used in the Old Testament?
- When are they described as part of God's law? When are they part of prophecy or poetry?
- How do these Scriptures speak to you?
- How do you think your circumstances might differ from the lives of the ancients? How are they the same?
- What is your response to God's call for a tithe?

When Jesus speaks, he does not negate the need for a tithe but rather insists that it must be given as part of a passion for justice and mercy. Consider how you and your church use the offerings for God's work in the world.

- What programs are important to you?
- How do they make a difference in your community? In the world?
- Do any of the passages you've read make you uncomfortable? comfortable?

- Are there certain passages that tell you that you are on the right track?

Exploring the Bible

To start your group thinking and talking about financial giving as a key part of discipleship, share with them as many of the enrichment Scriptures as you feel would be helpful to the group. Discuss:

- Have you ever felt frustrated by the feeling that some of the world's problems seem to be too difficult to eliminate?
- What encouragement have you found when you have ignored the naysayers and your own negative feelings and donated to the work of the church?
- What do you think Jesus is saying to those who criticize the woman for anointing him with expensive perfume?
- What does Jesus expect these onlookers to do? What does Jesus expect us to do?

Turn the discussion to the passage from Leviticus and the way it relates to Ruth.

- Since many of us no longer work on farms, what are some ways we can allow others to "glean" in our fields?
- What opportunities do we have, at church and elsewhere, to give to others?
- Since the Bible does not label giving as optional, how should this change our attitude toward our offerings in church?

If you attended Sunday school as a child, it's likely you've heard the story of the Widow's Mite found in Mark 12:41–44. Review the story and discuss:

- Have you ever felt that you have given all you have to the work of Jesus?
- Is there a loophole in what Jesus says?
- When have you heard this story in sermons? What has been the approach or message?
- What do you take from this story?

Mark 10:17–31 includes the famous passage about the camel and the eye of the needle.

- Have you ever heard a sermon about the eye of the needle that took an unusual and appealing approach? Do you feel that the approach was biblically sound? Why or why not?
- Why do you think there is a general reluctance to challenge people to give money to the church?
- What does Peter say in this passage in response to Jesus' statement about our chances of getting into heaven? How does Jesus answer? What does this text say to you?

Exploring the Book

In Chapter 5, Bob Crossman talks about the pastor who says that he baptized his parishioners' hearts but not their wallets. He follows this with a list of items that new members are generally asked to pledge when they join the church of Jesus Christ.

- What is your response when you hear a sermon or lesson on giving?
- How do you feel when someone preaches a sermon on giving that really challenges the congregation and deliberately seeks to make them uncomfortable?
- Imagine ways in which your congregation could be shown that giving isn't an unpleasant obligation but a joyful response to all that God has done for us.

Crossman talks about the challenge of raising our giving by one percent a year in order to achieve a tithe.

- Are you ready to pledge and step up to tithing?
- Is your passion for giving the same as your passion for prayer and daily Bible reading?

Take time to review the various personal stories shared in this chapter. Share your own stories of surprising results when you have given more than you thought you could afford.

- What did you decide to go without?

- How were you able to make up the difference in some of your obligations?
- How did you feel about yourself?

WRAPPING UP

Take time to read and remember the covenant made at the start of this series, which is posted in your meeting room. Review what the covenant says about generosity and financial giving.

Ask group members if they are ready to fill out the commitment card for financial giving this Sunday, and in so doing to praise God for all the gifts they received.

Claim the fifth step on the Committed to Christ journey. Commit to raising your giving by one percent over the previous year.

Ask the group to post on the wall the fifth of their six footsteps: "Financial Giving."

Closing Prayer
Read in unison

Giving God, grant us the strength to commit and follow through in our giving, with joy, and in our commitment to follow your Christ. Amen.

6.
HANDS-ON SERVICE IN JESUS' NAME

Goals

- Name and claim biblically why hands-on service in Jesus' name is essential for believers.
- Identify Scriptures that point to the centrality of service in the lives of believers.
- Recall and claim stories of individuals from the book and group members' own experiences.
- Lift up examples of how group members or church members have created significant ministries for your community or the global community.
- Recommit to the covenant shared in the opening session.

PREPARING FOR THE SESSION

Personal Preparation

Read Chapter 6 twice, carefully, and read the corresponding session in this leader guide between those readings. Take notes to help you guide others.

The activity involving the "celebration cake," if you choose to do it, will take extra work on your part. Make sure you make arrangements for you or one of the group members to take the lead in handling this element. See details below in "Materials" and "Opening Activity."

This is the final week of Committed to Christ. Think about all the ways that you and your group can remain committed in the weeks and months ahead. This week, think in particular about how your commitment to Christ will be exemplified in your hands-on service in Jesus' name.

Make sure you leave time before the session to gather all the needed materials.

Enrichment

James 1:27
James "the Just" was the brother of Jesus and the leader of the Christians in Jerusalem until he was murdered (stoned to death) by religious authorities in A.D. 62. His letter contains more echoes of Jesus' words than any other non-Gospel book in the New Testament. In his day, widows and orphans were those most likely to fall into the cracks and suffer, because they had no one directly responsible to care for them. James, the brother of Jesus, sums up practical Christianity in one sentence.

Psalm 118:24
In this psalm of thanksgiving, the songwriter praises God's creation and the privilege of our existence.

1 Corinthians 12
The apostle Paul emphasizes the need for everyone's gifts to be used in order for the church to be the body of Christ.

Galatians 5:13–16
Here, Paul quotes Jesus and the nineteenth chapter of Leviticus to help the Galatian Christians get along: One must love one's neighbor as oneself!

Matthew 25: 31–46
At the end of time, Jesus won't ask for a profession of faith; he will insist on a résumé of what you have done, for though you are not saved by your works, your faith is proven by your willingness to reach out to those on the margins of society, who seem to have been forgotten.

Materials

- Photocopies of the opening and closing prayers, as needed
- The final set of footprints made in the introductory session: "Hands-on Service in Jesus' Name"
- Tape or pins to fasten the footprints to the wall
- Six celebration candles
- A (pre-baked) "celebration cake" and frosting. Bring enough frosting to cover the cake in one color, and some frosting in another color to write on the cake, along with implements to frost the cake. (Be sure to provide a suitable alternative for those with allergies, medical conditions such as diabetes, or dietary restrictions such as those who must eat gluten free, have nut allergies, or who are lactose-intolerant.) Ask other group members in advance to bring additional refreshments, including something to drink, as well as plates and utensils.

LEADING THE SESSION

Opening Prayer

Light all of the six candles. Pray aloud:

All: Open our eyes that we may see you, Lord Jesus, when you are hungry, when you are thirsty, naked, sick, and in prison. Open our ears that we may hear the suffering all around us. Open our hearts that we may serve you by serving others: the dispossessed, the marginalized, and the poor, for in their eyes we see your eyes. This we pray in your name, Lord of the Nations, King of the Universe. Amen.

Introducing the Topic

Ask group members to review the commitments they have made over the weeks of Committed to Christ. How are the commitments going? Has it helped to offer support to each other in making and keeping these commitments?

In particular, ask group members to share any progress they have made regarding last week's topic, financial giving, by seriously restructuring their spending and their giving.

Opening Activity

Remind the group that this is the final week of Committed to Christ. Your church may be having a celebration following the service to review the past weeks of the program and to lift up the ministries of your church. Whether or not your church has chosen this option, your group deserves to celebrate the program and the new commitments that have grown out of it.

Present the pre-baked "celebration cake," unfrosted. Invite group members to frost the cake together. Then, as a group, decide how to decorate the frosted cake using the second color, and pitch in together to celebrate the program.

The group will be eating the cake at the close of the session.

Exploring the Bible

There seems to be a branch of Christianity (not confined to any one denomination or group) that dismisses the importance of active Christian ministry, locally and globally, by citing "salvation by grace, not by works," or perhaps sniffing disapprovingly about the "social gospel." But Scripture is very clear that faith without positive, visible, "hands-on" works is a dead faith.

Ask a group member to read James 1:27. Then discuss:
- How does James, the brother of Jesus, describe what real religion is like?

- Who are the people in today's world who would be most likely to be neglected and fall between the cracks?
- When have you been able to help those truly in need? When have you received help in similar circumstances?

The apostle Paul was constantly promoting good works, such as collecting financial aid for the poor Christians in Jerusalem. On another occasion, one of his good deeds was to pay the fees needed to release four Christians from a Nazarite vow.

Read aloud a passage from another one of Paul's letters: Galatians 5:13–14.

- Paul refers to the freedom given to us by grace; but what are we to avoid with this freedom? What do you think that means?
- How do you imagine the Galatians responded when Paul asked them to serve each other like slaves? How would you respond?

Paul quotes Leviticus and Jesus when he tells the Galatians to love their neighbors as themselves.

- According to Jesus, who are our neighbors?
- We usually think people should show gratitude when we do them a favor; but how does serving our neighbors as slaves change the way we should look at service in the name of Jesus?

Jesus describes the end-time judgment in Matthew 25:31–46. Nowhere does Jesus ask, "Do you confess me as Lord and Savior?" He seems far more concerned with whether individuals are engaged in ministry with the lowliest in society.

- What ministries of your church actively serve those on the margins of society?
- Do those ministries involve support at a great distance, or are church members actively involved?
- Which ministries are you involved in? Which ministries would you like to be involved in?
- What is the greatest need in your community? What would you define as the greatest need in the world community?

Exploring the Book

The author begins Chapter 6 with the marvelous story of Orville Kelly, who, after the initial shock following his diagnosis of inoperable cancer, told his family, "I'm not dead yet." He formed a club called MTC: Make Today Count.

Recite Psalm 118:24 together. Discuss the following questions:

- What have you done this week to make today count?
- Are there opportunities you passed up, at least for the moment, because you decided you could do them later?
- What are some things you can do going forward to make sure every day counts?

Later in Chapter 6, the author quotes his friend Jack, who said, "I can't sing. I can't teach. I can't speak in public. But I can sweat. If you ever need work done, I'm your man."

- What does it mean to "sweat," as Jack claimed he could do?
- What service have you done in the name of Jesus locally, or farther afield? What service are you best suited for? Take time as a small group for everyone to name and claim a talent. Invite group members to name the talents of each other as well. Write the talents on a large sheet of poster paper.

1 Corinthians 12 describes many different kinds of gifts, but one Holy Spirit, as well as how those gifts work together to help the church. Turn to Chapter 6 and lift up some of the types of service described.

- Which story of service was most interesting to you?
- Which story best matched your experience, or the skills you think you bring to the body of Christ?
- Is there one story that reminds you of someone in the group? Name that story and person.
- Look over the poster paper list you created, describing ways the group members "sweat." What skills do you think are missing from this list? Where can these be found in your congregation? How can you enlist individuals to use these gifts for the church?

The stories of Dan West (in Enrichment, above) and of Pat and

Tammy (in Chapter 6) are good examples of ways in which someone can perceive a need, fulfill that need, and organize others to work together in meeting that need.

- What needs do you perceive in your community, or in the larger world?
- What skills are present in your church to address that need?

Seriously consider whether now, or at some time in the near future, your group might work with the larger congregation or district to begin a ministry that fills a need. Set a date for your first meeting.

Close by inviting group members to lift up those stories from all the book chapters that you found most memorable.

- Why do you find these stories and characters most memorable?
- Do you see something of yourself in them?
- Do you see something of what you would like to be?

WRAPPING UP

Invite group members to discuss or recite the covenant from the opening session.

Claim the sixth and final step on the Committed to Christ journey. Invite the group to post their final footprints on the wall: "Hands-on Service in Jesus' Name." Take a moment to view all the footsteps on the wall and "walk" through the previous five steps.

Now ask group members to pause for a moment's reflection about their final commitment card this Sunday. Are they ready to serve and to make hands-on service in the name of Jesus a part of their commitment to the Gospel? Are they prepared to continue that commitment in the future?

Ask the group to consider which, of the six themes explored during the course of Committed to Christ, the group might like to study in more depth and detail during the coming weeks. Print out a copy of "Follow-up Resources" from the CD-ROM that accompanies the *Program Guide,* which includes good suggestions for follow-up study.

Share sentence prayers, offered by group members in no particular order. Focus on steps that lie ahead and the need for support and encouragement. The leader may close with a longer prayer.

Covenant to check in with each other on a regular basis. Set aside a time before or after worship, or on a special day during the week.

Encourage the use of social media, e-mail, and the phone as means to support and encourage each other.

Bring out the "celebration cake" again, and discuss all the commitments and opportunities that group members can celebrate. Cut the cake and serve the refreshments.

Closing Prayer (from Psalm 41:1, 140:12, 40:17, James 1:27)

Leader: Happy are those who consider the poor; the Lord delivers them in the day of trouble.

All: I know that the Lord maintains the cause of the needy, and executes justice for the poor.*Leader:* As for me, I am poor and needy, but the Lord takes thought for me. You are my help and my deliverer; do not delay, O my God.

All: Let us never forget. Religion that is pure and undefiled before God, the Father, is this: to care for orphans and widows in their distress, and to keep oneself unstained by the world.

Leader: Go in peace to love and serve the Lord, in prayer, Bible reading, worship, as a witness, in giving, and in service! Amen!